Trapped in My Body, in My Own Words

Claire Centrella

ISBN 978-1-64515-917-9 (paperback)
ISBN 978-1-64515-919-3 (hardcover)
ISBN 978-1-64515-918-6 (digital)

Christian Faith Publishing, Inc.
832 Park Avenue
Meadville, PA 16335
www.christianfaithpublishing.com

Printed in the United States of America

In loving memory of my daughter Melissa

Foreword

Meeting Melissa Centrella on the set of *Growing Pains* was one of the highlights of my childhood memories. She appeared to be beaming with excitement as *Growing Pains* was one of her favorite TV shows in the 1980s. She had come to visit as part of her wish to meet the cast and take pictures. When I saw Melissa sitting in the audience chairs on tape night, her smile was lighting up the room! As we posed for a quick picture after the show, she looked up at me with her big brown eyes (oh, those eyes!) and told me, "I love you!" Her mom gasped at Melissa's forthrightness. Melissa was anything but shy, always kind, always thinking of others, and one of the most beautiful human beings I have ever met. Over the years, Chelsea and I had the privilege of visiting with Melissa, Angie, and Claire, and their wonderful extended family of friends for birthdays and other celebrations. The parties were amazing... Everyone loved Melissa! In this beautiful book, you'll get to experience some of the stories, good and bad, that made up Melissa's miraculous life. Told from her mom's perspective, you will know from where Melissa got her big heart. My life is better because I knew Melissa. I'm almost convinced she was an angel in disguise (I think I saw her wings once...) and I'm excited for you to get to know her too!

Kirk Cameron

Lynn Imperiale

Preface

Tribute to Melissa

This tribute of Melissa's life was a compilation of stories she told her best friend Angela while growing up. There are memories describing her beauty for life from special friends and family. Celebrities whose lives she touched have remained in their hearts forever. In her mom's loving words, with heartfelt emotions, she brings her daughter's life alive with stories, poems, and quiet moments of reflection. Her best friends Angela, Sal, and I were privileged to be asked to share this special tribute with you. Once you read and see her beauty, she will never leave you. She will be stamped in your life forever as a beautiful ballerina that dances in your hearts when you need that little nudge to go on. Melissa, this one's for you.

Lynn Imperiale

Special thanks to Claire Centrella, Angela Guerriero, Sal Balsamo, and all the people who have contributed to Melissa's book.

About Dystonia

Dystonia is a little-known and complex life-altering brain disorder. The symptoms include excessive, often painful, muscle contractions that cause involuntary movements, postures, and disability. Dystonia is a thief, robbing those affected of the ability to control their own bodies, walk without falling, or grasp a cup and bring it to their lips, hold up their heads and make eye contact during a conversation, keep their eye lids open to drive, or speak easily and be understood. The disorder affects men, women, and children of all ages and backgrounds.

Dystonia is the third most common movement disorder with conservative estimates suggesting it affects at least 250,000 people in the USA, but experts really do not know how many people are affected. Because understanding of dystonia is not as widespread as it could be, even obtaining a diagnosis can be very challenging and can take more than five years. Dystonia may be misdiagnosed as an orthopedic condition, cerebral palsy, essential tremor, a tic, or muscle cramps.

There are many forms of dystonia; the disorder can appear very different from one person to the next. Dystonia may affect a single area of the body or multiple areas throughout the body. The movement symptoms may be chronic or occur only periodically. Oftentimes, dystonia will worsen with a specific task. For example, hand dystonia symptoms may arise only when writing or playing a musical instrument. Dystonia may occur by itself or with other abnormal movements like tremor. The age at which symptoms begin may influence prognosis and treatment. Dystonia that begins in childhood is more likely to involve multiple body parts and more likely to be associated with additional movement and neurological symptoms. Dystonia that develops in adulthood is more likely to remain focal to a specific body area.

There are many causes for dystonia. Dystonia may occur due to an inherited or new genetic mutation. Dystonia may also result from changes in brain activity caused by another health condition like Wilson's disease, Parkinson's disease, or a traumatic brain injury. Certain drugs are known to cause dystonia. One of the many frustrating aspects of dystonia is that for many people who develop dystonia, there is no identifiable cause.

Because there are many types of dystonia and diverse symptoms, the treatment must be specific to a person's individual needs. Treatment may include a combination of oral medications, botulinum neurotoxin injections, and/or surgical procedures such as deep brain stimulation (DBS). Many people use a *sensory trick* to temporarily relieve a symptom with a gentle touch on a specific part of the body. Complementary therapies may include occupational therapy, physical therapy, speech/voice therapy, pain management, and other therapies depending on the person's symptoms. It is also critical that the non-motor symptoms of dystonia, including depression and anxiety, be treated.

The Dystonia Medical Research Foundation (DMRF) was founded in 1976 by Frances and Samuel Belzberg, parents of a young woman with dystonia. They, like Claire Centrella, have worked tirelessly for decades to make sure people have the support and resources they need to manage life with dystonia while the DMRF supports cutting-edge research toward improved treatments and ultimately a cure. These special individuals acutely understand the heartache dystonia brings to those affected and to their families and friends.

The board of directors of the DMRF is comprised of volunteers who are personally affected by dystonia. Many have dystonia themselves while others have loved ones living with dystonia. The DMRF takes very seriously its responsibility to those who are affected by dystonia and waiting for relief. The Foundation's leadership believes the ultimate service the DMRF can provide the dystonia community is a cure. In the meantime, education, advocacy, and support programs are available while dystonia researchers continue their important work to cure dystonia and end the need for the DMRF.

Thank you to Janet Hieshetter for providing this information. For more information on dystonia or the DMRF go to www.dystonia-foundation.org or on Facebook at @dystonia.foundation or at 312.755.0198.

In My Daughter's Eyes

"In my daughter's eyes, I am a hero. I am strong and wise, and I know no fear. But the truth is plain to see: She was sent to rescue me. I see who I want to be in my daughter's eyes."

—Martina McBride

Tribute

In my daughter's eyes, I saw a beautiful young woman—although trapped in her body—full of life, love, and goodness. She never complained, always caring about others. I saw a strong-willed person, totally dependent on others yet never angry. She had more love and admiration for me than I deserved. I saw fear, pain, and suffering on her face yet a true acceptance of her life. She had hope of getting better while having fears of getting better because she might not be able "to live in this world" being sick so long.

Melissa appreciated the littlest things in life. With an unwavering faith, she would say, "Mommy, I have a good life." I can never forget someone so beautiful inside and out who had a maturity far beyond her years yet had a pureness unmatched by anyone.

Melissa was the daughter I always hoped for. There is nothing she wouldn't discuss with me nor anything I felt uncomfortable discussing with her. I would know what she was thinking before she said it. We loved all the same things and were best friends.

Not long before she died, she said to me, "Mommy, I admire you."

And I said, "Missy, why?"

She continued, "You work, pay bills, take care of me and Daddy, work for dystonia, and help everyone. I just admire you." I told her no one could say anything nicer to me. I guess she wanted me to know. On the last day of her life, her heart rate dropped to fifty and held there until I got to the hospital. A soon as I entered, her heart rate went to zero, and the nurse said, "She waited for you." She held on until I returned.

In my daughter's eyes, I saw everything I wish I could be.

Melissa, this is my tribute to you. I love you and will always be so proud of who you were. I miss you every day.

Mom

Her Story

*M*elissa *Anne Centrella's story is that of the triumph of the human spirit. Though her physical abilities became increasingly limited in her battle with dystonia, there was nothing that could ever break her will to live as full a life as possible. It was because of this that Melissa's story has continued to reach and inspire so many, including those within the world of entertainment.*

Sal Balsamo's Eulogy to Melissa

She was most definitely an angel because when you sat and talked with her, you understood why we need to be good to one another.

It isn't an explainable feeling, but when you left her, your heart was softer, your mood more mellow, and your demeanor was calm.

In her presence, we were all on our best behavior.

We never spoke out of line and for some reason, we always minded our manners.

Her constant barrage of *please* and *thank-you* had us all a little unsettled because we saw in her the way that we all should be.

She was pure and loving.

She offered all of us encouragement in everything that we did.

Time with her was a reminder that you weren't doing your best to be as kind as you could to others, especially those closest to you.

This is because she set the bar for what it meant to live.

Erase from your mind, for one minute, the physical nature of her being and ask yourself: Who else would you rather be like?

The purity of her heart showed brightly in everything that she did and in every conversation she had.

We should all be envious of how easily it came to her.

Her polite nature engulfed you as her loving aura illuminated the space that you shared with her.

Was it solely me who noticed that the only person who didn't feel sorry for Melissa was Melissa? How often do we get down about the slightest missteps our life may take?

Yet our remarkable friend accepted the circumstances of her life and was determined to move ahead.

To her, her pain, the physical pain that was beyond words and all of the emotional pain her circumstance afforded her, was simply a fact of life.

To her, this was her life, and she never let it impede her determination to make the most of it. Yes, she was ill, and she conceded her body to disease—but not her mind, her heart, nor her will.

She was determined to fight so long as she could so that she could enjoy her life on her terms.

She was definitely a harbinger of peace because she had her pain, yet she had so much hope and faith.

She was faced with guaranteed pain for an undetermined amount of time, yet she endured with faith and love—completely void of bitterness.

That is indeed true peace.

That is a peace I pray we all find. She never allowed her illness to define who she was and neither should we. We will all miss her.

But we can find her in our hearts.

If we paid attention to who she was and noticed what kept her strong, then our hearts have changed. And her impression has been made.

Like I said, she was an angel with a pure heart and love of life.

Strength

"Anyone can give up, it's the easiest thing in the world
to do. But to hold it together when everyone else would
understand if you fell apart, that's true strength."

—Evangeline Love

Description of Her Physical Condition

Description of Melissa's Physical Condition:

Initially, Melissa would just hold her left arm bent at the elbow at the age of six, and we were told it was a habit. At seven, she started to drool and was diagnosed with dystonia. By August of that year, she began to fall when she would turn, and by year's end, she was in a wheelchair. She continued to progress to a walker, wheelchair, motorized wheelchair, and then bed. Her hands got so spasmed that she no longer could use the motorized wheelchair. Because the doctors were afraid she might get pneumonia, they decided to do a Nissen wrap which would inhibit her ability to cough or vomit.

By the ninth grade, she had difficulty staying upright too long in a wheelchair and had to be home tutored for the last couple of years of high school. She graduated from high school and slowly became more and more bedridden. She was the first patient to get Botox in her legs, face, and arms. She was the first patient to receive an intrathecal pump under her skin in her stomach, which administered morphine and baclofen to the spine and up to the brain in a continuous fashion. She was overdosed with medication and was in a coma for three days at the age of sixteen. At one point, she was on 100 mg. of valium which the doctors said would kill an elephant.

She had seizures and was on Tegretol, and a local doctor stopped it. And then she went into a grand mal seizure. That was the beginning of the end. She then, because of severe pain after the seizure, had to have her gall bladder removed, and was put on a respirator. Shortly after that, she had pneumonia and was on five antibiotics intravenously. She couldn't stay on the respirator any longer and they did a tracheotomy. On June 4, 2002, she passed away.

Melissa had secondary dystonia, which means she had a primary disease which caused the dystonia. When she was originally diagnosed, we did not know this. Dystonia was relatively new to the medical world, and the movement disorder group told us she would progress and eventually only be able to crawl. She was tested for Wilson's disease, Hallervorden-Spatz, and other possible illnesses. A muscle and nerve biopsy was performed to determine if it was Leigh's disease but could not find mitochondria that matched. One doctor was certain it was Leigh's disease and the other was not. Leigh's disease usually is from the mother, but recent DNA testing showed Melissa's mom was not a carrier.

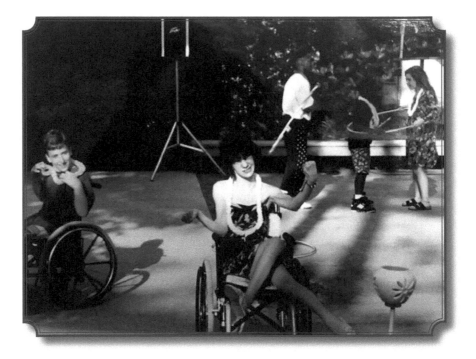

First Memories

"Take care of all your memories.
For you cannot relive them."

—Bob Dylan

Birth

Who: Melissa Anne Centrella
What: A girl
Where: Holy Name Hospital, Teaneck, NJ
When: February 21, 1977
Parents: August John Centrella and Claire Ann (Triggiano) Centrella
(married)
President: Jimmy Carter

Melissa's Own Words

Toys—I had a doll that I was fascinated with. When you push a button on her back, it (stretches) and her teeth grow in. When you push another button, she goes back to the way she was. I still have that doll somewhere.

Parents, grandparents, great-grandparents—When I was younger, my grandma and I were so close. My grandma used to take me to school and back. My mom and dad were working, so my grandma was the only person who could take care of me.

Holidays—(6/5/98) I have spent six holidays in the hospital. Easter, Thanksgiving, Christmas day, New Year's Eve, and New Year's Day. But even though I was in the hospital for those holidays, it was still good having my family and friends with me.

Hobbies—Some of my hobbies include watching TV, reading books, or magazines. I collect Barbie dolls, makeup (all kinds of makeup), Precious Moments statues, teddy bears, and all special kinds of goose eggs (they are cut out in the middle). They have something like a carousel horse or glass slippers. I also collect pictures.

The accomplishments of which you are the most proud—(6/5/98) Of having my mom and dad like I have.

Fashions—Since I was young, I always loved to wear fancy dresses. I always liked to be all dressed up. I love bright colors, and I love to make an appearance with my clothes (and I have to always match).

Famous people you have met—For the past couple of years, I have met a number of celebrities such as Kirk Cameron, Chelsea Noble, Rosie O'Donnell, Ann Jillian, everyone from *Full House* and *Saved By the Bell*, and soon to meet Celine Dion.

Have you grown in spirit?—From the time I was seven, I've had to grow up very fast because of being in and out of hospitals and watching other people do what I couldn't.

7/19/98—One time, my mom said I was seven years old going on forty because I didn't act like my age.

Persons who have been a special influence in your life—My mom. Everything I ask my mom for—not material things but stuff that is impossible—my mom makes possible.

Gifts, special gifts you have given or received from special people—My parents gave me the best gift of all, life.

Children and the things they say—When younger, I was in church with my parents and was speaking when I was not supposed to and got caught. After arriving at home, I said to my mom, "I'm going to my room." My mom didn't have to say anything. My mom was trying to potty train me, so one day I said to my mom, "I went poo poo," but she didn't believe me until she looked in the toilet.

My mom was surprised and happy and gave me a hug and said, "Good job."

Food—(6/5/98) From the time I was very young, my dad had told me to try everything. I ate almost everything from sushi to liver. I love vegetables.

Influence of music and dance—When I was younger, I took ballet lessons. Ballet was my life, and then my mom said that I might have to stop because of the dystonia. The color pink reminds me of ballet because most ballerinas wear pink.

Brushes with physical danger—One time, when I was in the hospital due to overdoses of medicine, I was in a coma for three days but when I woke up I was back to myself.

Unforgettable people you have met—(6/5/98) Mr. Walker, school principal, is a tall African American gentleman. He's so loveable and so caring. He's just a nice guy. Mr. Ryan who was a good friend of mine and was also an English teacher.

Lessons you have learned—(6/5/98) Never let anybody take your dreams away from you.

Tears you have shed—(6/5/98) I have shed a lot of tears over dystonia.

Vacations and other trips—(6/5/98) I've been to five states on vacation: Massachusetts, Connecticut, Georgia, California, and Florida. At each one I've been to, in my mind I remember bits of each one.

Changes—I've been through a lot of changes, from having to be able to walk and take ballet, to being in a hospital at the age of seven, and then, at the age of eight, being in a wheelchair.

Your own fairytale—(6/5/98) My twenty-first birthday to me was definitely like a fairytale come true. It all started on February 22, 1998. I woke up at ten-thirty. My mom's beautician came and did my hair, and when she was done with my hair, my mom's friend put makeup on me. And Anna, my friend and helper, put my gown on me (and Chelsea). A good friend of mine agreed to be my date.

Melissa's Own Words

"Never let anybody take your dreams away from you" (6/5/98)

"My job's not done."

Caring

"Never believe that a few caring people can't change
the world. For, indeed, that's all who ever have."

—Margaret Mead

This is about my very special friend who is an angel here on earth. I have yet to find a fault with her. She is beautiful, intelligent, compassionate, loving, patient, kind, and I could go on and on…

I love Melissa with all my being. She is with me all the time. I carry her in my heart. Whenever I think of her, I smile, and I feel loved. I am very lucky to have someone *so* special in my life.

Joyce Woodall

Struggle

"Life imposes things on you that you can't control, but you still have the choice of how you're going to live through this."

—Celine Dion

Melissa's Own Words

"My life today has gotten a lot tougher now. I need help almost with everything, Now it's even harder because I am getting older and I know that my life won't be the way it was when I was younger. And I see that I missed out on a lot of great things in life."

Humility

"A meaningful life is not being rich, being popular, or being perfect. It's about being real, being humble, being able to share ourselves and touch the lives of others."

—Unknown

Melissa's Own Words

"My parents gave me the best gift of all—life."

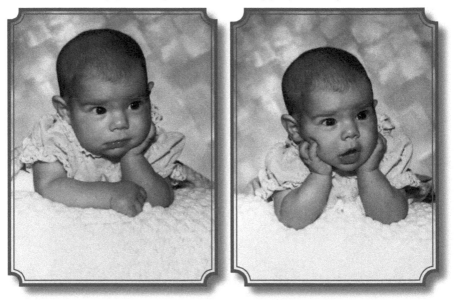

Inspiration

"When I stand before God at the end of my life, I would
hope that I would not have a single bit of talent left
and could say, I used everything you gave me."
                                        —Erma Bombeck

My granddaughter Melissa is such an inspiration to all. In spite of all her pain and suffering, she always has a smile. If you ever asked Melissa how she felt, she'd always say, "I feel great!"

Dystonia is a progressive disease, especially the kind Melissa has. It affects the whole body. I remember when we first heard of dystonia, we didn't know anything about it. It would break your heart to see how terrible that sickness really is. When I look at Melissa, it really hurts to see her suffering so much for all these years. I pray that, soon, there will be a cure for dystonia.

Grandma Terry Triggiano

Read at Melissa's Funeral Mass

Everyone who knew Melissa knew that she was an angel. She was very caring and wanted only the best for her friends and family. She always told them how proud she was of them. And she was always concerned about the health and happiness of those whom she loved, even as they were taking care of her. As a tribute to Melissa, we should try to celebrate her caring nature and spirit every day in our own lives.

Since it is said that music is the song of angels, it is fitting that her spirit be celebrated with a song. As a tribute to her spirit, this song is for all of us here today.

"The Prayer," composed by Carole Bayer Sager and David Foster.

I pray you'll be our eyes and watch us where we go and help us to be wise in times when we don't know... Let this be our prayer.

Angela Guerriero

Melissa's Own Words

Lourdes—"Mommy, I wouldn't know how to live in this world if I got better. And if I didn't what would I have to hope for?"

7/19/98—"My mom and dad inspired me to reach for my goals and to never stop hoping, praying, and dreaming."

For My Special Mommy

Written to the Today Show for a Mother's Day Contest
4/22/98

Dear Sir,

I am having someone write this note for me as I am handicapped and cannot write anymore. I'm bed bound and since I was seven years old was diagnosed with a neurological brain disorder called dystonia. It started with my left arm involuntarily going up/rising, pain, and spasms and has gotten much worse.

I am writing to you because I would like to let you know all the wonderful things that my "special mom" has done to make my life worth living! Let me start why my mom is special to me. My mom has always been there for me and at my side. She has tried to bring the world to me since I cannot really get out into the world. She has tried to keep my spirits up by making me "fly high." So far, my mom has made my every wish come true! I asked her if I could meet Kirk Cameron, and as hard as it was, she made it happen. A couple of years ago, while I was in the hospital in New York, I was accidentally over medicated and temporarily in a coma. My mom stayed by my bed, holding my hand, and praying. She asked all her friends to pray for me, and three days later, I woke up! Another time, when I was in the hospital, I wasn't able to eat anything, and my mom was so nice because she would eat on the other side of the room not to make me feel bad. She stayed with me day and night in the hospital for five months out of eight, but she got sick due to her nerves. You see, my dad is sick too, and my mom supports us all by working very hard!

My mom also is the president of the Northern NJ Dystonia Chapter because I asked her to help with a cure so no one has to suffer in their life like me. I don't think there's too much to be done for me, just nice doctors and help for pain at times. Dystonia has kind of taken my life, but my mom gives it back every day to me just by loving me so much and trying to put some beautiful things and people into it! My mom also wrote the most beautiful poem about me which was published by The Poetry Guild. *I am enclosing it for you to see how special she is and the love she has for me.*

For the life my mom has given to me, I would like to do something special for her to return my love for her. It's difficult for me to do this in my condition, so I'm asking you to help me if you can. My mom has not been away since I was seven years old, and I'm twenty-one now. She's always dreamed of going on a cruise. I know this because I watch her face and her smile when a commercial comes on the TV. She's never wanted to leave me, but I know I'm strong enough to stay with my dad and friends and family to let this happen. I want to put some happiness and joy into her life like she has put in mine. Here is a picture of my special angel mom who God has bestowed upon me. You can see the love in her smile at the twenty-first birthday party she gave to me… Again, her name is Claire A. Centrella.

Thank you and all my love!

Melissa Centrella
Love you, Mom!

Blessing

"A miracle is really the only way to describe motherhood and giving birth. It's unbelievable how God has made us women and babies to endure and be able to do so much. A miracle indeed. Such an incredible blessing."
—Jennie Finch

"Melissa, Our Blessing"

Claire A. Centrella

My new, sweet baby girl,
With big black olive eyes,
Has our heads in a whirl
With the ultimate highs.

She's growing so fast,
And the years are flying by.
Now eight years have passed
In a wheelchair—God why?

Now twenty and bedridden,
Filled with love, faith, and hope,
Melissa touches many—
Helping everyone to cope.

What is the reason
For this pain and cross?
To enjoy each new season
And never feel a loss.

The hopes and dreams at birth
Of a life that might have been.
But none can more be worth
What God turned into a win.

Published by *The Poetry Guild*
December 1997

Failure and Hope

"I don't pray for God to take my problems away, I pray only
for God to give me the strength to go through them."
—Jose Lozano

In Melissa's Own Words

*I*n my lifetime I've been through a lot of ups and downs. Sometimes
I think I've been through more downs than ups and other times
when I look at all I have I know that I've been through more ups."
In 1998 my mom has found a new medicine that's been tried out on
rats that had strokes and have been paralyzed. The medicine had proved

the rats had gotten better. My mom
told me that I'm so young and I still
have time, for the medicine might
work on people and it might work
on me.

*Another time when I was in
the hospital I had an awful time.
My whole body was moving and
I was talking differently. That
night, when I went to bed, I asked
my mom to tell everyone that she
knows to pray for me. The next
morning, I was a lot better. I
think that it was a miracle."*

Unconditional Love

"Tears are prayers too. They travel to God when we can't speak."
—Psalm 56:8

"I Am Loved"
Melissa's Song

God gave me life,
And I felt so loved.
What more to want
But grow in faith?
And then the unexpected came—
A life of pain and suffering,
Wheelchair and bedridden.
But God and love, always there.
So I missed what others
Took for granted.
God's love was always there.
Tears, fears, hopes, and prayers—
Every emotion one could feel.
What more to want?
I live my life with few regrets
Because I know I am so loved.

Friendships

"Some people arrive and make such a beautiful
impact on your life, you can barely remember
what life was like without them."

—Ann Taylor

She was sweet sixteen. It was the first day of school. I was going to meet Melissa for the first time, and I was nervous. She didn't know me, and I was hoping she'd like me. To my surprise, we hit if off right away. It was like having another daughter. She was open, friendly, sweet and surprisingly frank. I found her totally refreshing. I was her instructional aide assigned to accompany her to all of her classes, assist her at lunch and to her personal needs. What the school didn't realize was that the assignment became a labor of love. You see, from that moment on, Melissa became a part of me and my life for which I will always be grateful.

We began to slowly understand one another. When Melissa and I would be in the restroom, I would blend three different shades of lipstick to get the "right look" for her. Melissa loved to match colors and had exquisite taste in clothes. Everyone would always comment on her outfits. She matched from head to toe, and of course, the lipstick was very important, as was her beautiful hair.

She's very artistic and would love to design T-shirts. She came over to my house on several occasions, and we would make shirts and accessories. She also loved to cook, so we would make some wonderfully fattening dessert and eat it all! We shared the love of chocolate so it wasn't hard picking something good to make.

When I would visit her at home, we always went through fashion magazines together, talking about the latest trends and styles. She loved to be read to so we did that often too. She was always full of questions about people and wasn't afraid to share her thoughts. I especially liked when she honestly told me my hair was too blonde that month or I needed to freshen my makeup. Her candid style was what made her so special. She shared a rare gift of viewing life from a perspective few of us will ever experience. She knew how precious each day was and always thanked God first for each and every day.

Melissa had an infectious laugh. When she got going, it was hard for anyone not to giggle along with her. She loved to hear stories about families and happenings in the school to which she graduated. Her keen instinct about people was uncanny, and her memory of teachers and friends would surprise many who did not know her. She could remember the smallest detail of stories I forgot I've even told! It didn't matter to Melissa that people are different. She loved meeting and making new friends and would be the most loyal friend you would ever have. She understood the complications of life and would quickly remind you that life was a blessing and to cherish every moment.

I have cherished every moment, thanks to Melissa. She has been my greatest inspiration and friend. So many lives have been enriched because she has been part of them. To all of you who read this and knew her, lucky are you to have been in her life. For all of you who haven't had the extreme pleasure of her warmth, laughter, and love, I hope this book has touched your lives and reached your souls to help you view every day the way Melissa did…with a heavenly blessing!

I love you Melissa.

To my "babe" always,
Lynn Imperiale

When you first meet Melissa, it is so hard not to be amazed at how positive she is. Along with seeing how thoughtful and polite she is, you also find out immediately what a beautiful person she is. There are not many people that are like her. In life we are faced with disappointments and heartache. Melissa has been handed more than her share of both, yet she has come to terms with it and has excelled at looking to more positive light. The first time that I was able to spend some real time with Melissa, it was like I had been introduced to an entirely different way to look at life. After the first time I was able to talk with her, my life changed for the better. She makes me, and I'm sure everyone else she meets, want to be better.

There are parts of life that seem like a big deal and they really are not. She has shown me that life is not about things but about people and that you can help to make them feel better about themselves. For Melissa, life is not about herself but other people. She cares so much for not only the people she sees regularly but also people she has only met once. She wants things to go well for everyone else and she worries about herself last. Given her situation, this type of attitude is remarkable and, above all, admirable. She is perhaps the most pure person that anyone could know.

I am so thankful that I have Melissa as a friend. She is so understanding. Melissa hears what is bothering someone and immediately thinks about what she can do to make it better. If she doesn't have a solution she has a caring and kind word, which from her can be just as good or even better. Being Melissa's friend is so rewarding. From her kind words and caring heart, from her positive attitude and happy-to-see-you smile to the goodness that she radiates, Melissa is truly a special person. I am so thankful she is my very best friend. Everyone should be so lucky.

Sal Balsamo

Melissa was an inspirational human being. From her early age, she was a happy, cute little girl who was interested in everybody who approached her. As she grew older, her difficulties, challenges and even suffering grew greater, but she also evolved into a more generous and spiritual young lady. During the eighteen years or so that I had the privilege of seeing her, I never heard her complain about her enormous suffering and difficulties. On the contrary, she was always smiling at all her friends and visitors, always inquiring about all our family members and always "happy to see you." It appeared that *you* were more important than her, while, in fact, we were visiting to see her and to show her our concern for her situation.

Melissa was an angel on earth. Her concern about others was constant and she never asked for anything other than to enjoy the treats her mother Claire would offer her by visiting actors and actresses, by bringing her to shows, and by collecting beautiful dolls.

An angel on earth is what Melissa Centrella was. I remember her always and I pray *to* her.

Manuel Boado.
New Rochelle, NY

M is for Melissa, an angel from above
E is for eternity, God's greatest gift of love
L is for the light that shines
In all she's here to do
S is for her smile—simple, sweet, and true
So full of love, so full of life
All that we learn from you

C is for Camp Firefly, where memories we hold dear
E is for her energy, never showing fear
Never giving up
Trusting in God's plan
Radiantly does she shine; a lesson for all man
E is for her essence, elaborate sense of flair
Lacey socks, crimson lips, and
Long black flowing hair
All that you are is all that we love; you are God's living prayer.

Melissa Centrella, I love you!

Barbara & Robert Cameron

I met Melissa and her family early in my teaching career as she came to a self-contained classroom of special needs students in a building that was handicapped accessible. It was a challenging setting for her gentle soul because she was typical in every way but physically limited, needing help in the bathroom and with communication. Melissa didn't have learning or emotional issues, and her classmates did. I believe this is where her deep compassion and empathy for others began as she watched her new friends struggle with various behavioral, social, and academic problems. Melissa quietly counted her blessings. She realized she was fortunate to have loving parents and a stable home and all her needs met before tackling the demands of a school day. Many of her peers didn't always come prepared, and this was upsetting to her. Sharing a small classroom with ten others creates a family atmosphere, and I can remember her offering to share her snack or lunch frequently. Brave Melissa didn't seem to dwell on her own troubles as her motor abilities declined and she struggled each day with walking, eating and talking. Her muscles were not cooperating with her and in the years we were together she became wheelchair bound and relied on her aide Lynn to communicate.

Missy had developed a strong relationship with a boy in the class that was very sweet on her too. He was hard on the outside due to his circumstances at home but found relief at school and in his friendship with Melissa. These two kids were only about ten years old, but each carried the weight of the world. Her friend ran away from home one night... Melissa was distraught at the thought of him being scared and alone out in the dark world. She called me and insisted that we had to find him.

"We need to help!" she urged as I grabbed my keys to go looking. Hours of driving around and a call back to say that I was unsuccessful and ask if he had contacted her had Missy in tears about how unfair life was to him. To him... It was never about her. Melissa always counted her blessings in life. She amazed me every day. I can still hear her snorting laughter.

Melissa graduated from elementary school amidst the cheers of parents and students. She insisted to be on the stage in her chair while others stood singing. With help, she proudly stood as her class was called to be congratulated smiling broadly!

Ellen Wolf

Melissa was a very special friend who had given me the direction in my life that I had desperately been searching for. As long as I can remember, I was always trying to figure out why I was here on earth. I remember being a little girl praying in church on Sunday, asking God for my purpose. I never expected to figure it out not at least this early in life but I think I finally got an answer.

There was a time in my life when I could not find happiness within myself. I could not find anything to fulfill me. Then, one day, I met Melissa. She showed me that there was a purpose in my life. I cannot explain the joy I feel when I make her smile or laugh. After spending more and more time with her, I started to realize that I did have a purpose, and that was to be a loving and caring human being who helps others. Melissa has been the greatest example for me, one that I hope to become for others someday. She has taught me to put others first and to enjoy the simpler things in life because more times than not those are the things that count the most. I don't know if I could ever be as strong as Melissa, but she has taught me to face life's challenges and get through them without giving up.

I've never met a person with so much love in their heart. When I am with her I have such a good feeling inside. I can't think of anything else in this world that makes me feel this way. She is like an angel who was put on earth to show us the way. She shows people the meaning of life and love. A visit with Melissa always brings me back down to earth, and I always leave with a feeling that I am doing the right things with my life.

Now I know that I am here for a reason, and I have a very special person in my life that I can always count on to remind me of that. She has shared her love with me and has made me a part of her family. I don't think I could ever repay her for what she has given me, but hopefully she knows how much she has done for me and how much I love and care for her. I certainly would not be the person I am today without her. She has been my inspiration and my guide to become a better person. I thank God every day for allowing me to be part of her life. She is truly a gift from God.

Sharon Drost

Dear Melissa,

Thank you for your sweet note. We were in Canada shooting our next movie for a month and just came home. I wanted you to have this CD & tape. Enjoy.

The CD was Ann singing "The Wind Beneath Your Wings."

Love & God Bless,
Ann & Andy (Ann Jillian)

Melissa's Eternal Fortitude— One Battle to Be Conquered by Many!

It's hard to put into words the exuberant amount of spirit that Melissa shares with everyone she touches. Even when she began to encounter many physical constraints because of illness, Melissa's mental and spiritual abilities became even stronger. When she came upon the hardest challenge of her life, Melissa continued to keep herself in good spirits by always showing there is a positive outlook on everything. She never showed signs of giving into this devastating disease that has hit her so hard.

Melissa has blessed this world with her presence as a child of God, providing an extremely enviable impression that will last throughout many generations.

Melissa's gift goes beyond the display of her own abilities. Melissa has instilled in her closest friends and relatives the need to help others with this debilitating disease. By doing so, her mother Claire established the Dystonia Medical Research Foundation's New Jersey chapter. Melissa's continued strength in fighting the disease has surely affected many others, bringing them together for one common cause—to carry the torch and lead the fight for a cure.

Melissa is a loving daughter, grandchild, niece, cousin, and friend. She will always be in all of our hearts and prayers.

Melissa, our love and admiration for you will be everlasting. Even though we may not always be physically present, you can rest assured that our hearts and prayers are forever with you. May God bless you, enabling you to continue to share your perpetual love and devotion with others.

Love,
Uncle Rob, Aunt Sue,
Bob, Danielle, Brian, and David

Melissa and I hit it off the first time we met. In spite of her illness, her engaging spirit to those around her was evident. She was a treasure to behold. You always felt honored in her presence.

Your forever friend,
Barbara Heiser

Future

"Nothing is more beautiful than the smile
that has struggled through the tears."

—Demi Lovato

In Melissa's Own Words

"I can't really think about the future right now because now all I think about is what will happen to me tomorrow. It's hard to think about what's going to happen when…"

Bravery

"Be Brave. Do not pray for the hard thing to go away. Pray for a bravery to come that's bigger than the hard thing."

—Ann Voscamp

Some Thoughts from Mom (7/14/17)

Melissa had so many challenges in her short life:

- Was over dosed with Baclofen and was in a coma for three days
- Went down to 77 lbs. and was like someone who was malnutritioned. It caused stomach bypass and couldn't eat by mouth for 5 months. She used to ask me to eat so she could watch me. OMG
- Had to get stomach bypass
- Had to get esophagus wrap so she wouldn't get pneumonia
- When she was about twelve (after trying the traditional medical route and all nontraditional approaches such as cupping, crystals, etc.), I asked her if she wanted to go to Lourdes. She stopped and thought about it and said, "No, Mommy. If I got better, I wouldn't know how to live in this world, and if I didn't get better, what would I have to hope for?"
- Went in for deep brain stimulation, and they shaved her head, put the halo screwed into her head, and then said they couldn't do it. They never checked the MRI in advance. She cried and cried, and they rushed us out of the hospital by noon. That seemed to be the beginning of the end. Hospitalized in January. Passed away on June 4.

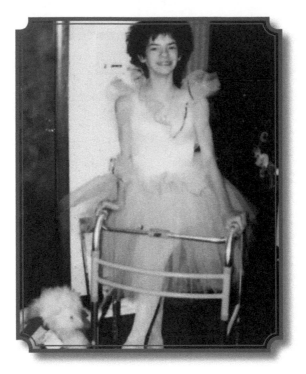

June 4, 2002—Mom's Thoughts the Day Melissa Went to Heaven

As I sat in the hospital on the last days of Melissa's life, I prayed to the Blessed Mother since I knew she understood the pain of watching her only son die at such a horrendous and young death.

And I said, "Dear Mary, you at least knew he was the son of God." And then I thought, *Well, I know Melissa is a daughter of God.*

Then I thought, *Yes, but you knew your son positively changed the world with all his good works.*

And again I thought, *Melissa has too positively changed the world in so many ways.*

- She brought people together to pray over and over again in God's name.
- She taught people to see the good in life no matter how it might be.

- She suffered for years with dignity and courage without complaints.
- She always worried about everyone else and prayed for others before herself.
- She encouraged people to say "I love you," who probably rarely did before, because she was always saying it first.
- She taught people to say "I am sorry" because she was sorry for things that she had nothing to do with.
- She loved, prayed, suffered, cared, showed courage, and faith, and always with dignity.

So, yes, my daughter Melissa was very much like Jesus in her own small way. And I believe we were fortunate to have been chosen and blessed to have her in our lives.

Melissa, now it is your time to rest in peace and love with the Lord. Please pray for us because we will always be praying for you.

Frequently Asked Questions

1. Schooling/barriers/acceptance—Be your child's advocate and speak up. Ask what is provided, and make sure they comply. There are laws to protect you and your school should provide the necessary accommodations including a barrier free environment.
2. Medical insurance/state offerings—Apply for Medicare if your child is disabled, and if your child is eighteen, you can apply for Medicaid.
3. Nursing/Live-ins—Some great resources would first be your church, friends, recommendations, and (last choice) an agency. Be sure that your child is comfortable with your choice. Be ready to change if they don't make a good fit. Sometimes the task is difficult and one person can become overwhelmed and stressed on both sides. It may be advantageous to consider multiple aides to meet your needs.
4. Agencies—Research several and ask that they have alternates in case they cannot fulfill an assignment if they cannot make the visit. Determine if you need an aide or nurse as well.
5. Physical occupational therapy—This should be supplied by the school.
6. Hospital specialties and doctors—Research the hospitals near you who specialize in the particular illness of your child. Don't always rely on local hospitals for special needs.
7. Foundations—One great organization for advocacy and research is NORD (National Organization for Rare Disorders). Other smaller organizations can deal with specific illnesses. Join them and support them.
8. Support for caregiver—Remember you will need help as well. The caregiver needs respite and support to be able to help your child. One can only be a good caregiver if they care about themselves first. Take care of you.

Epilogue

Scholarship Foundation

She had a dream and a passion for helping others...

Melissa Centrella was a Nutley High School Graduate and resident of Kinnelon, NJ. Melissa left us in June of 2002 after a twenty-year battle with dystonia. This scholarship will serve as a tribute to Melissa's life of courage and love.

In the fall of 2002, Melissa's friends and family gathered to create a scholarship fund in her honor. Melissa's life was a remarkable one. Having left her impression in the hearts of all who met her, we feel that it is now our turn to carry on her mission. Her mission in life was simple in name and complex in deed. Hers was a mission of love. Without question the purest heart known to those who met her, Melissa made it her life's work to help others, particularly those afflicted with dystonia. Through her mother Claire, Melissa put her energy behind many charitable causes. With her actions and words Melissa inspired everyone she met to be the best that they could be. It is with that same energy that her family and friends have gathered to award several yearly scholarships to students with the same characteristics as her.

Each year, The Melissa Anne Centrella Scholarship will be awarded to students in New Jersey, pursuing a career in nursing, medical sciences, or a medical technical field. Because medicine and care were so important to Melissa's everyday life, she had a deep respect for the people that helped to bring dignity, comfort, and respect to her special needs. The board members know that Melissa loved to help people. In turn, The board has decided to award scholarships to students who hold the same care and respect for others that Melissa had. Students applying for the Melissa Anne Centrella Scholarship will have to display a record of volunteer work for consideration. After all, it was Melissa's many sacrifices that made her the special person that she was.

We have expanded our foundation in memory of Melissa by adding to the scholarships. Melissa's Hope also awards needed donations to families with a disabled child or children each year. Donations have included a new wheelchair, a trip (vacation for the family), money to help pay medical bills, etc. The recipient will be chosen from recommendations submitted by friends and families of the Centrella family. We know that Melissa would be thrilled to see us helping those handicapped children in need. Our website is https://melissashopenj.org/

To make a donation by check or money order, please send to the following address:

Melissa's Hope
c/o Mrs. Claire Centrella
3124 Dillon Court
Toms River, NJ 08755

About the Author

Melissa wanted her story to be told and did so by asking her friends to write down her thoughts. Many of her friends, family, and teachers shared their thoughts as well. Melissa was an inspiration to everyone showing unbelievable courage, strength, faith, and love. I know she hopes that this book is an inspiration to everyone who reads it.

CPSIA information can be obtained
at www.ICGtesting.com
Printed in the USA
BVHW022107230719
554217BV00015B/121/P